The
Mindfulness
Activity
Book

Michael O'Mara Books Limited

First published in Great Britain in 2022 by
Michael O'Mara Books Limited
9 Lion Yard
Tremadoc Road
London SW4 7NQ

A CIP catalogue record for this book is available from the British Library.

Papers used by Michael O'Mara Books Limited are natural, recyclable products made from wood grown in sustainable forests. The manufacturing processes conform to the environmental regulations of the country of origin.

ISBN: 978-1-78929-422-4 in paperback print format

1 2 3 4 5 6 7 8 9 10

Cover design by Claire Cater
Designed and typeset by Gareth Moore

Featuring colouring pages by: Angelika Scudamore, Anna Shuttlewood, Claire Cater, Jo Taylor, Julie Ingram, Katrin Alt, Pimlada Phuapradit, Sam Loman, Emily Hamilton, Jake McDonald, Jasmine Burgess, Lizzie Preston, Andy Naidu, Lizzy Doyle

Printed and bound in China

www.mombooks.com

Introduction

Sit back and relax with this book packed from cover to cover with mindful puzzles and activities. Whether your idea of a break is to solve a sudoku or simply to peacefully colour in a picture, this book has you covered. Or if you'd prefer to try a word puzzle, then give the word searches and crosswords a go.

Try to start by clearing your mind of the day's distractions, and focus on just the task in hand – so that nothing exists beyond the page that's right in front of you. Once you have your pens or pencils, you're ready to go and everything else you'll need can be found within the bounds of this book.

You could start your mindfulness session with one of the spot the differences, dot-to-dots or mazes – these puzzles will require just enough focus that you are paying attention to the task, but not so much that they'll feel like work!

Or, if you fancy a real challenge, then try the bumper-size hanjie puzzles. These reveal hidden pictures as you solve them, based on the clues around the grid. See below for full instructions.

The puzzles are not arranged in any particular order, except that the later spot the differences have more changes to find, and a couple of the final hanjie puzzles are even bigger than the rest. Where needed, solutions are given at the back of the book.

Have fun, and enjoy the puzzles!

Hanjie instructions
Shade some squares according to the given clue numbers. The clues provide, in reading order from left to right or top to bottom, the length of every run of consecutive shaded squares in each row and column. There must be a gap of at least one empty square between each run of shaded squares in the same row or column.

Sudoku instructions
Place a digit from 1 to 9 into each empty square, so no digit repeats in any row, column or bold-lined 3×3 box.

Solution on
page 113

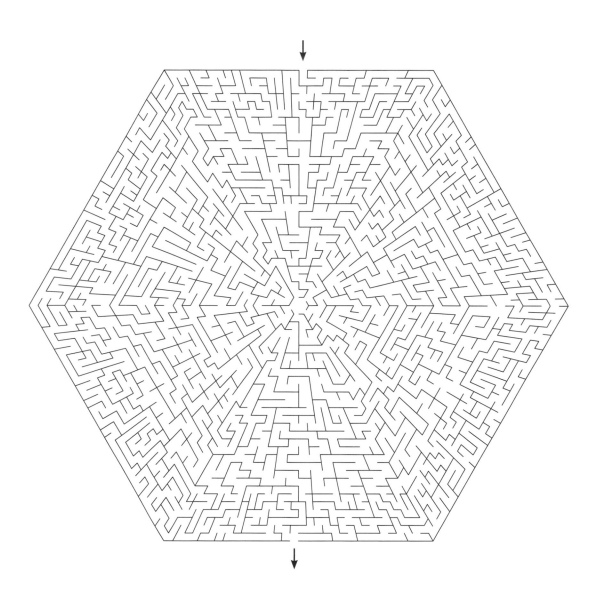

There are 10 differences to find.

Solution on page 113

2			8		7			1
		7				6		
	9			4			2	
9			4		3			8
		8				4		
4			2		9			3
	4			2			5	
		9				8		
6			3		4			7

Solution on page 113

			4		6			
	4		3		7		8	
		8		5		6		
4	8						5	9
		6		1		4		
7	2						6	8
		2		7		5		
	9		2		1		7	
			5		3			

8: Hanjie

Solution on page 113

Picture clue: Flaming hot

Column clues (top to bottom):

```
                                          3        2
                                          2  2     2  5           3
         2        2     2               5 1 3 2  3  3  2  4        2  2
      5  1  1  4  5  4  5  4  1     1    3 1 3 3 5 5  4  3  5  2  2  2  3  4  3  3
      2  6 15 13 10  3 10 13 16  4  1  1 1 3 3 5 1 2  4  1  3  1  3  2  2  3  3  6
      8  1  2  3  6  6 15  6  6  3  2  1 1 2 14 8 1 2 4  4  1  2  1  2  5 11  2  2  7 15
```

Row clues (top to bottom):

- 3
- 5
- 1, 1, 1, 1, 1, 1, 1
- 5, 1, 1, 1, 2
- 2, 2, 5, 1, 1
- 3, 1, 2, 1, 2
- 3, 7, 1, 2, 1
- 9, 1, 1, 2, 2, 2
- 2, 1, 1, 1, 4, 1, 1, 1
- 1, 1, 6, 1, 2, 2
- 9, 1, 2, 1, 1
- 1, 7, 5
- 2, 7, 9
- 1, 8, 4, 8
- 1, 8, 5, 3, 6
- 1, 8, 4, 3, 2, 4
- 1, 8, 3, 3, 2, 2, 2
- 1, 8, 1, 4, 2, 2, 3
- 10, 1, 3, 2, 4
- 2, 7, 1, 3, 3, 1
- 1, 1, 1, 2, 4, 1
- 1, 1, 1, 4, 2, 1
- 1, 1, 1, 2, 3, 1, 2
- 1, 1, 1, 2, 4, 1, 3
- 7, 2, 2, 3, 5
- 2, 2, 2, 2, 4, 2
- 2, 2, 2, 2, 2
- 3, 3, 2, 2, 2
- 4, 4, 2, 2
- 5, 5, 2

9: Colouring

10: Spot the Difference

There are 10 differences to find.

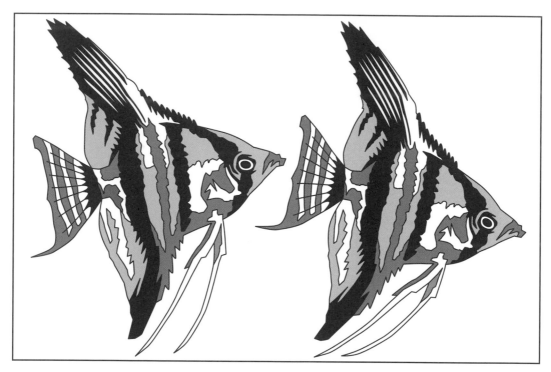

11: Wavy Maze

Solution on
page 114

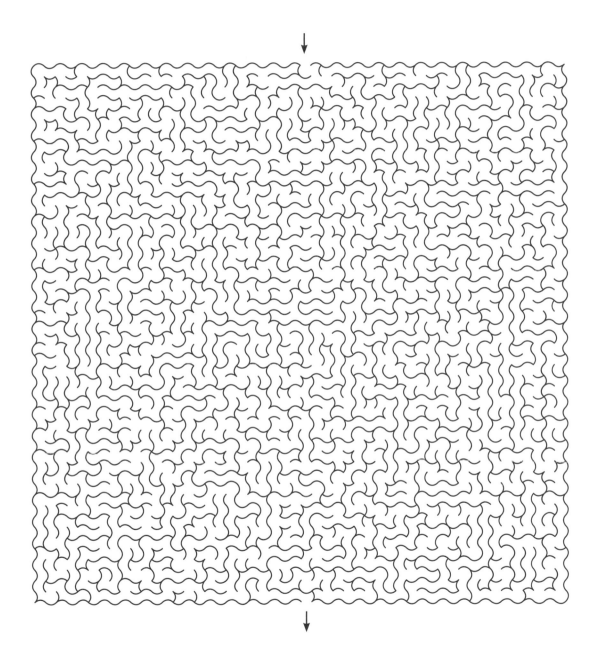

13: Spot the Difference

There are 10 differences to find.

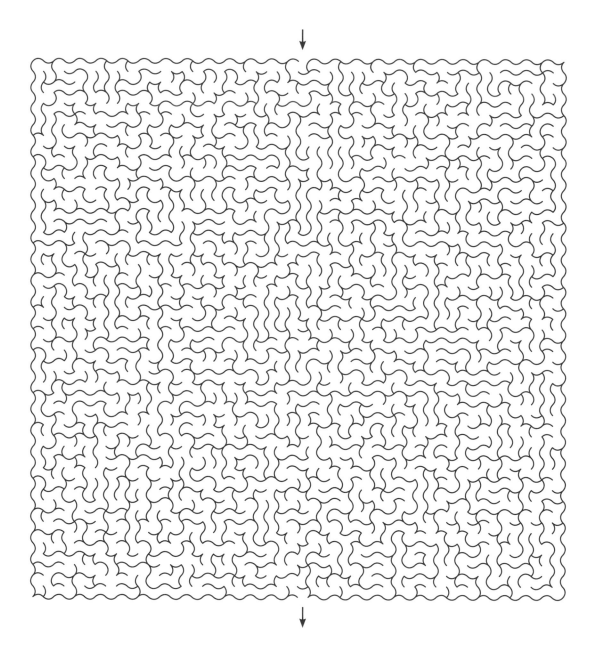

Join dots in increasing numerical order, starting each path at a star. Lift your pen each time you reach a hollow circle.

17

Solution on
page 114

Join dots in increasing numerical order, starting each path at a star. Lift your pen each time you reach a hollow circle.

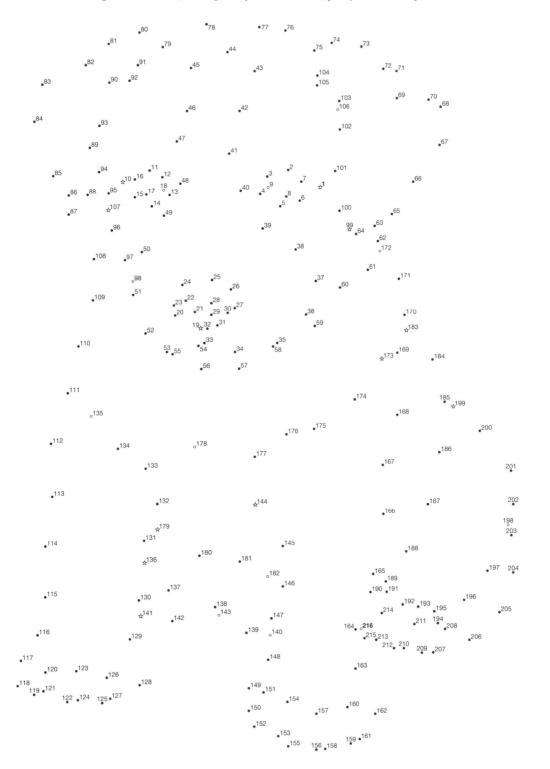

Join dots in increasing numerical order, starting each path at a star. Lift your pen each time you reach a hollow circle.

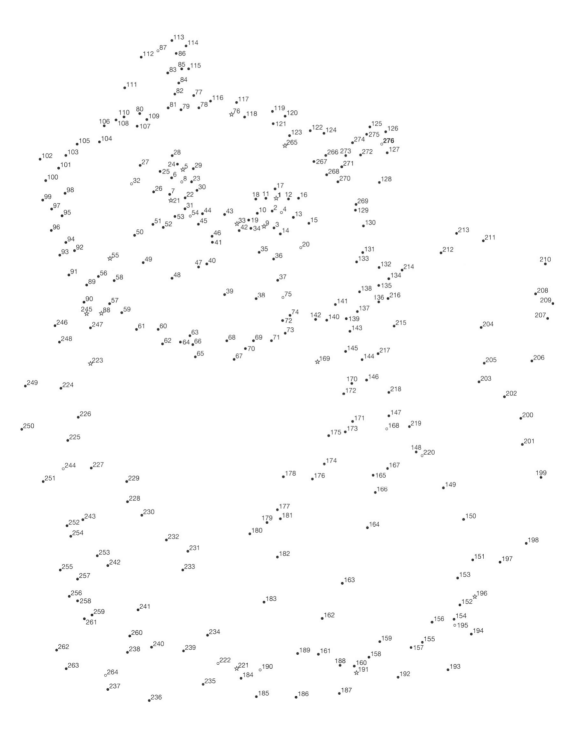

21

Solution on
page 115

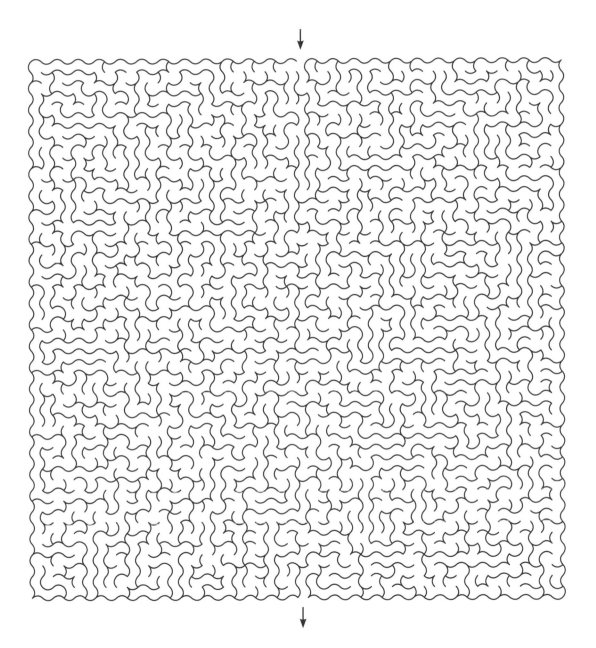

23: Square Maze

Solution on page 115

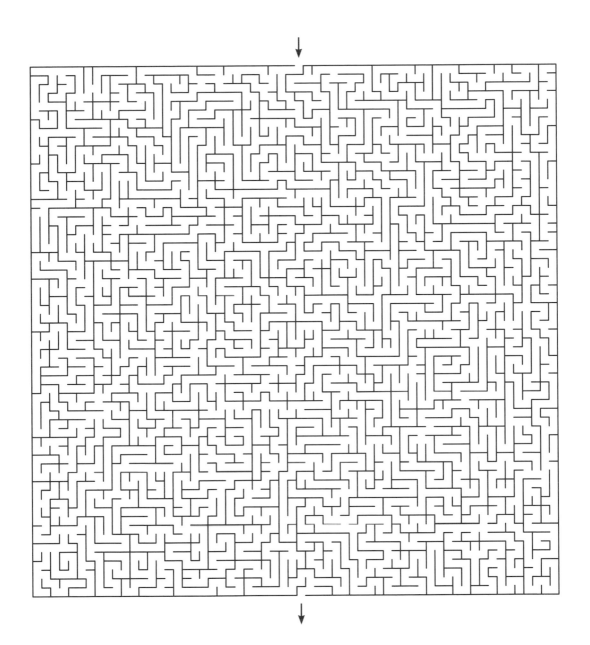

Solution on
page 115

Join dots in increasing numerical order, starting each path at a star. Lift your pen each time you reach a hollow circle.

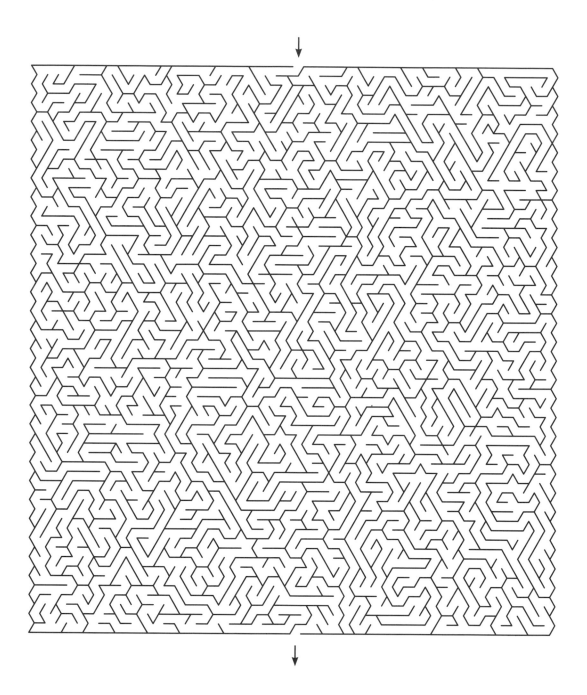

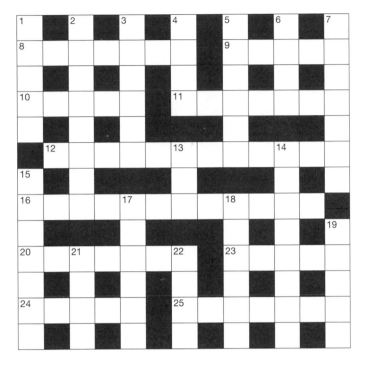

Across
8 Wandering over a wide area (7)
9 Anxiety (5)
10 As one, in music (5)
11 Soothe (7)
12 Futile (12)
16 Impresario (12)
20 Conforming (7)
23 Window-cleaning implement (5)
24 It may be Bengal or Siberian (5)
25 Mass books (7)

Down
1 Make a speech (5)
2 Natural impulse (8)
3 Surroundings (6)
4 Gelatinous, seaweed-derived culture (4)
5 Dining furniture (6)
6 Shivering fit (4)
7 Completely (7)
13 Mongrel (3)
14 Criminal activity (4,4)
15 Accounts (7)
17 Asylum seeker (6)
18 Most recent (6)
19 Sweep (5)
21 Side (4)
22 Pastes (4)

28: Stress Relief

```
S B S G I I W R I T I N G N G
M A N I N N E C G N I W A R D
S G G A U I G G N I C N A D G
B E A O G O M E C R G S O N N
I L O R Y G S M U N E I C N I
H T D G D I N N I T C G A S H
C N G B N E N I A W N A G I C
I I N G O I N L B I S N T N T
A I I G N X I I H M I L I N E
T N K G E P I G N T I N L E R
G Y L G R H U N T G L L N T T
T G A N R A G I G A O I C I S
N I W H L G N G G N I L C Y C
O I X E E K A E R O B I C S R
C L G N I Z I L A I C O S A M
```

AEROBICS
BOXING
CLIMBING
CYCLING
DANCING
DRAWING
GARDENING
KNITTING
LAUGHING
PILATES
RUNNING
SINGING
SOCIALIZING
STRETCHING
SWIMMING
T'AI CHI
TENNIS
WALKING
WRITING
YOGA

30: Hanjie

Picture clue: Puzzling

Column clues (top):

```
                4                    4                        1 1
          3 11 16 16                 5                     1  2 1
    5 7 7 7  1  1  2 12      12 16 16 5 3 1 1 1 3 2    2 3 5 2 1 3
    1 1 1 9  1  1  2  4       4  6  6 6 7 7 7 5 3 18   18 3 6 5 5 11
    2 3 1 5  1  1  2  2 10 8 10 2  2  1 1 18 15 15 15 15 1 17 17 17 1 15 7 6 6 7
```

Row clues (left):

4, 4, 1, 1	
4, 4, 2, 2	
5, 10, 6	
5, 5, 1	
3, 9, 3, 3	
19, 2	
19, 1	
19, 1	
19, 1	
19, 2	
13, 3, 5, 3	
11, 7, 1	
6, 6, 7, 1	
5, 5, 7, 1	
4, 4, 5, 1	
7, 18	
1, 15	
1, 15	
1, 15	
4, 18	
1, 2, 16, 1	
1, 15	
1, 15	
1, 2, 16, 1	
4, 18	
1, 15	
1, 15	
6, 9, 6	
2, 2, 2, 5, 5	
2, 1, 1, 6, 6	

32: Hanjie

Picture clue: Beach view

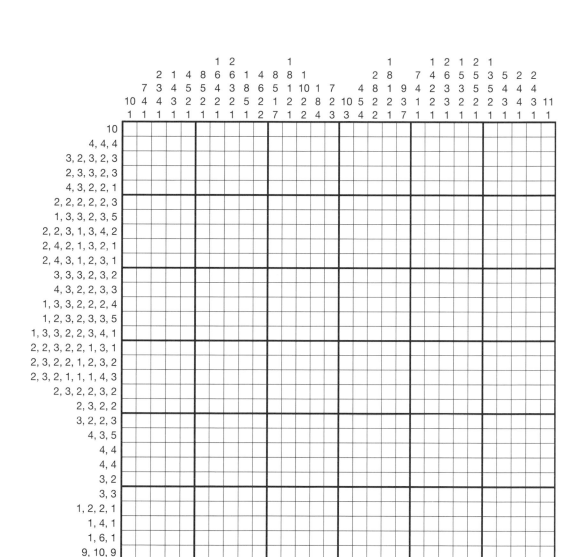

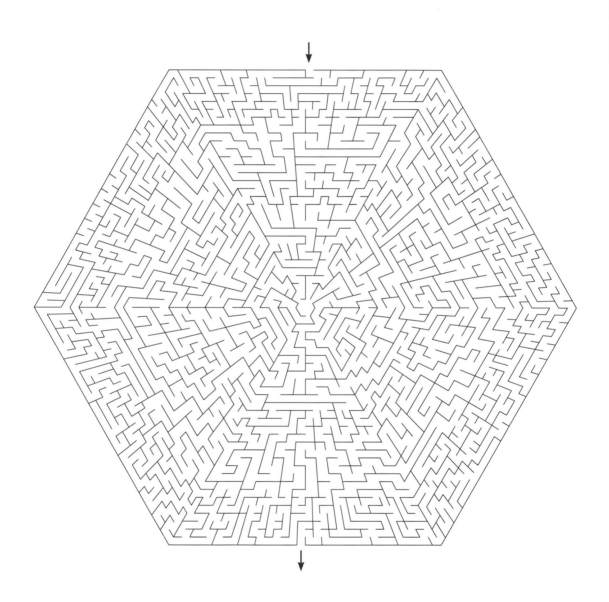

34: Spot the Difference

There are 10 differences to find.

Solution on page 116

	9			7			2	
6			9		3			1
			6		4			
	6	4				1	8	
1				4				2
	5	2				3	7	
			7		9			
8			2		5			6
	2			6			3	

37: Sudoku

Solution on page 117

			9		3			
		9		1		7		
	2	6				4	3	
6				3				5
	1		5		6		9	
9				2				4
	3	4				2	1	
		1		5		9		
			1		7			

38: Hanjie

Picture clue: Up and away

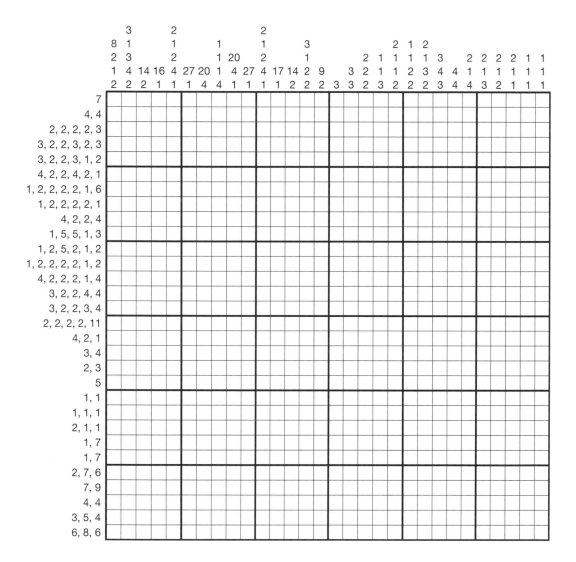

Across
1 Periods of time before events (4)
4 Plot outline (8)
8 Attractive (6)
9 Programming (6)
10 Cat sound (4)
11 Within the body (8)
13 As contrasting as can be (5,3,5)
16 Compassion (8)
19 Strokes gently (4)
20 Mammary duct opening (6)
22 Coiffure (6)
23 Coffee shot (8)
24 Corrosion (4)

Down
2 Almost, but not quite (9)
3 Relating to parody (7)
4 Engraving tools (5)
5 Enthusiastic (7)
6 Common birch-family tree (5)
7 Small hotel (3)
12 Settled ways of thinking (9)
14 Oscar category, 'Best ___' (7)
15 More cheery (7)
17 Daily news journal (5)
18 Rude and noisy person (5)
21 All the details: ___ and outs (3)

41: Peaceful Views

```
M D S P O R D N I A R S S M S
N E G E S I R N U S T E S T L
A P A W R U I R E A V N H I A
C O R D O Z N V O A O G N N M
I C D E O O A S E W I O N C I
F S L T E W D L E L N L A E N
T O N E P E G L N T L S W N A
N D H K L N R R A A A O S S G
R I I A I D E I F N B Z M E N
B E L L O H N R F N D A L S I
E L L O T S E A I G E I D M P
D A E R R T S A C R O N A O E
F K O A A F R A T E G L H K E
A N T W W G R S W L L P O E L
E S E L N Z E N G A R D E N S
```

CANDLE
FALLING LEAVES
INCENSE SMOKE
KALEIDOSCOPE
LAKE
LOG FIRE
MEADOW
NORTHERN LIGHTS
RAINBOW
RAINDROPS
SLEEPING ANIMALS
SNOW
STARS
STREAM
SUNRISE
SUNSET
WATERFALL
WAVES
WOODLAND
ZEN GARDEN

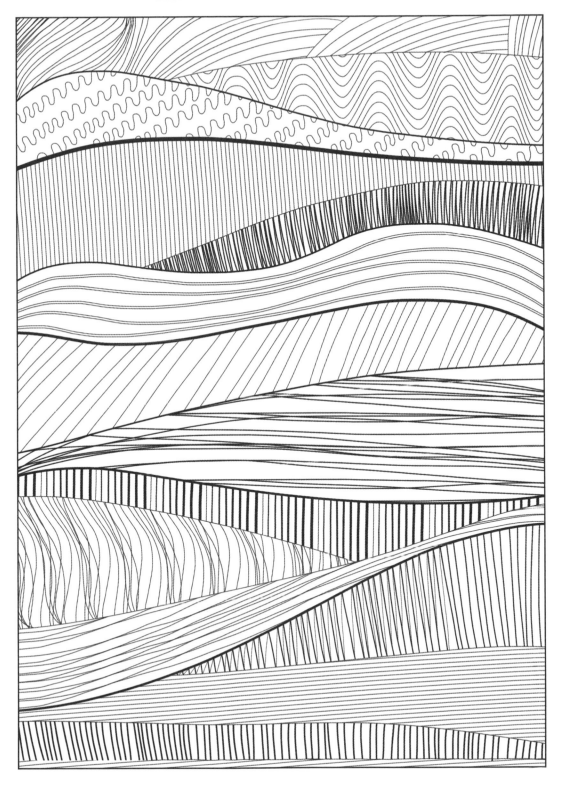

Solution on
page 117

Join dots in increasing numerical order, starting each path at a star. Lift your pen each time you reach a hollow circle.

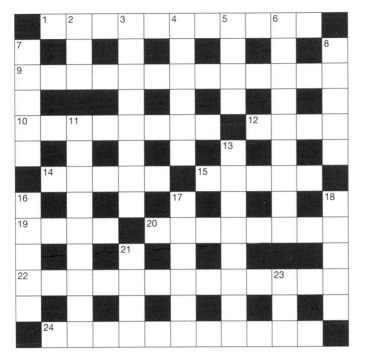

Across
1 Get to work (7,4)
9 Ambitious and go-getting (4-9)
10 Having plenty of spare time (8)
12 Lazy, perhaps (4)
14 Bird-related (5)
15 Related to sea-based military (5)
19 Direction to look to see the sun rise (4)
20 Extends (8)
22 Middle Ages contagion (7,6)
24 Overhaul, as a piece of equipment (11)

Down
2 A score of zero (3)
3 Shared, as in facilities (8)
4 Suds (6)
5 Self-important person (4)
6 Taken out (9)
7 Sacred song (5)
8 Summed (5)
11 Unable to be seen (9)
13 Fail completely (4,4)
16 Words that say what is happening (5)
17 Drew over using thin paper (6)
18 Buffoons (5)
21 Facts (4)
23 Slime (3)

T	L	B	L	H	E	R	B	A	L	T	E	A	D	P
L	T	W	H	O	T	S	T	O	N	E	S	E	E	R
E	N	I	M	R	O	P	C	L	Y	R	N	L	S	M
X	E	L	A	I	P	P	A	D	Y	O	A	O	T	O
F	M	L	B	R	N	R	L	R	I	I	E	H	R	O
O	T	D	O	U	O	E	M	R	W	I	L	I	E	R
L	A	G	E	O	R	M	R	A	I	Y	C	D	S	M
I	E	O	R	T	P	C	A	A	N	H	D	O	S	A
A	R	R	L	E	O	E	S	T	L	I	W	O	H	E
T	T	L	M	B	N	X	G	Y	H	W	C	T	B	T
I	E	L	A	I	C	A	F	N	D	E	A	U	O	S
O	O	I	C	E	R	O	O	M	U	O	R	T	R	S
N	T	P	O	A	N	U	A	S	A	L	B	A	E	E
R	E	E	G	A	S	S	A	M	A	O	P	U	P	R
I	N	A	E	R	U	C	I	D	E	P	N	I	S	Y

AROMATHERAPY
BODY SCRUB
BODY WRAP
CLEANSE
DE-STRESS
DETOX
EXFOLIATION
FACIAL
HERBAL TEA
HOT STONES
ICE ROOM
MANICURE
MASSAGE
MINERAL WATER
PEDICURE
PLUNGE POOL
SAUNA
STEAM ROOM
TREATMENT
WHIRLPOOL

	4						3	
1	7						5	8
			6	3	7			
	1		3		4	2		
	5			2		4		
	2		7		8	9		
			2	9	3			
3	5						2	7
	6						1	

4				8				7
	8		3		7		9	
		9		4		8		
	2						7	
9		7				1		2
	6						8	
		1		2		4		
	9		4		6		3	
7				3				6

Solution on
page 118

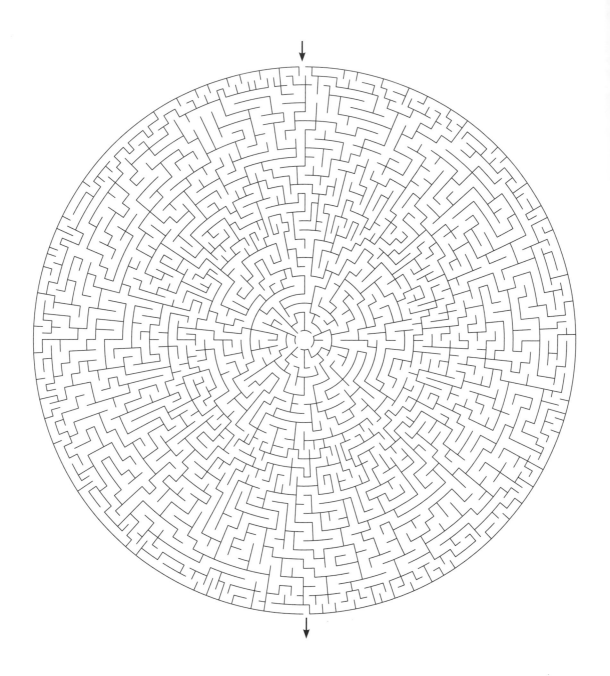

Across
1 Muscular (5)
4 Greatly frighten (7)
9 Absolute ruler (8)
10 Professional charges (4)
11 Maintenance (6)
12 Flip over (5)
13 A particular one of these (4)
15 Umbrella spoke (3)
16 Anthem (4)
17 Bright (5)
19 Intertwine (6)
21 Denoting 'half' (4)
22 Fresh; different (8)
23 All together (2,5)
24 Banded ornamental stone (5)

Down
2 Fit out (5)
3 Comes into bloom (7)
5 Make a humiliating apology (3,6,3)
6 Hurriedly search (5)
7 Liberty (7)
8 Readying activities (12)
14 Ex-celebrity (3-4)
16 Legally owned property (7)
18 Inner self (5)
20 Seashore (5)

I	T	E	Y	A	I	B	A	E	R	S	M	J	N	A
F	E	O	S	T	R	E	A	Y	M	A	O	P	G	I
T	U	O	E	N	S	B	N	U	E	B	O	N	E	E
H	D	I	O	U	C	N	I	A	A	N	I	S	H	V
O	E	P	Y	T	U	N	E	A	N	O	I	E	R	V
R	P	A	H	P	I	H	D	E	A	B	O	A	V	O
F	V	T	S	J	R	E	E	I	I	A	S	E	I	T
A	P	N	I	E	R	I	M	R	D	H	B	T	I	S
I	T	U	T	N	R	S	T	A	N	U	R	A	V	A
A	S	E	N	V	T	E	D	H	V	A	R	O	N	L
H	D	S	R	L	E	N	C	I	V	R	V	O	F	V
A	F	N	E	R	E	E	A	O	M	I	M	R	Y	E
T	S	M	R	T	A	R	A	U	D	O	E	R	A	N
I	P	N	M	E	M	E	Z	N	P	Y	V	T	P	I
O	A	N	M	A	S	E	O	N	R	I	I	C	O	T

ABNOBA
AGNI
ARTIO
ASH
CERES
DIANA
EOSTRE
FREYR
IOUNN
LEMPO
MEDEINA
POMONA
PRITHVI
SUIJIN
TAPIO
TERRA
THOR
VARUNA
VAYU
ZEME

54: Dot to Dot

Join dots in increasing numerical order, starting each path at a star. Lift your pen each time you reach a hollow circle.

Across
1 Unpleasantly pungent (5)
4 Formal address (6)
10 A person's innate timer (4,5)
11 Clod (3)
12 Rolled rice dish (5)
13 Equilibrium (6)
14 Not lasting (11)
18 Spread to (6)
20 Pallid; blanched (5)
23 Really warm (3)
24 Transmit (9)
25 Procession of people (6)
26 Sweeps along, like a cloud (5)

Down
2 Writes a computer program (5)
3 Slant (7)
5 First-class, informally (5)
6 Natural wearing-away (7)
7 Lift or carry (4)
8 Treat cruelly (5)
9 Intake (11)
15 Computer display (7)
16 Wandering (7)
17 Bodily sacs (5)
19 Flowed back out (5)
21 Gold star, eg (5)
22 Vessel (4)

56: Feeling Calm

C	D	C	V	A	D	E	I	F	I	N	G	I	D	D
O	E	E	N	L	L	I	T	S	A	L	D	T	E	F
L	L	S	T	S	P	L	R	E	I	E	L	D	S	L
L	L	D	P	N	T	O	D	E	S	O	A	H	R	U
E	O	E	E	I	E	E	I	O	L	E	N	U	R	T
C	R	E	A	S	T	T	P	S	H	A	P	S	C	R
T	T	Q	C	W	U	M	N	L	E	D	X	H	E	A
E	N	U	E	I	O	O	E	O	I	D	E	E	E	N
D	O	I	F	C	A	V	M	C	C	I	N	D	D	Q
H	C	E	U	Q	E	T	A	I	D	T	V	D	D	U
V	F	T	L	L	R	L	E	L	N	S	I	E	N	I
U	L	E	U	L	P	L	L	A	I	A	A	O	R	L
D	E	I	R	R	O	W	N	U	S	U	U	T	A	D
A	S	S	E	N	E	R	E	S	T	E	D	Q	U	H
P	C	A	P	R	I	V	A	T	E	C	E	D	E	Q

AT EASE
COLLECTED
COMPOSED
CONTENTED
DIGNIFIED
EQUANIMOUS
HUSHED
LEVEL-HEADED
PEACEFUL
PLACID
POISED
PRIVATE
QUIET
RELAXED
RESTED
SELF-CONTROLLED
SERENE
STILL
TRANQUIL
UNWORRIED

Solution on
page 119

Join dots in increasing numerical order, starting each path at a star. Lift your pen each time you reach a hollow circle.

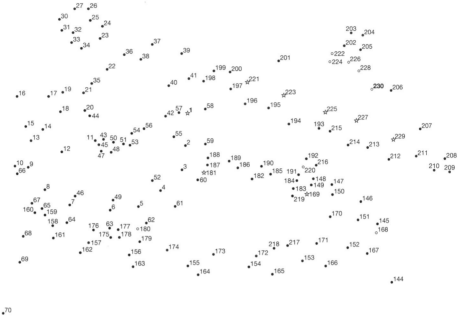

Join dots in increasing numerical order, starting each path at a star. Lift your pen each time you reach a hollow circle.

Across
1 Visual (7)
5 Animal flank (4)
10 Inexpensively (7)
11 States firmly (5)
12 Dance music (5)
13 Hindu retreat (6)
15 One who belongs to a group (6)
17 Womb resident (6)
19 Come up with (6)
20 Burning stick (5)
23 Roasting meat (5)
24 Computer (7)
25 Fairground amusement (4)
26 Deceiving (7)

Down
2 Spoken songs (5)
3 Reforms (12)
4 Regardless (6)
6 Outside; unenclosed (4,3)
7 Egg-laying location (4)
8 Specialist school (7)
9 Related to the science of numbers (12)
14 Spiral ear cavity (7)
16 Humanity (7)
18 Musical speed reversion (1,5)
21 Rule as monarch (5)
22 Not fully closed (4)

61: Feeling Positive

```
O E S L U F R E E H C E E N G
C E S E R U H N C L L M D L S
T D S S L O E O H B E E A D S
S N M N P F N T A A G A I H E
H E E E I V P T I A P S N D L
P A F D I A R O R N E P E L R
S U R N I O T U S L I C Y P A
L Y C D F F O R F S I F R B E
R E U M Y C N A E S E C E P F
D L O C N I S O I C O S I D N
F C E E E S G V C C S S S L C
M L A C U O E S E C U R E E E
M S O R O C O M P O S E D D D
E U E D A O P T I M I S T I C
E D P T N A I L E R F L E S T
```

CALM
CERTAIN
CHEERFUL
COMFORTABLE
COMPOSED
CONFIDENT
CONVINCED
DECISIVE
DEFINITE
ENCOURAGED
FEARLESS
GOOD
HAPPY
HARDY
HOPEFUL
OPTIMISTIC
SECURE
SELF-ASSURED
SELF-POSSESSED
SELF-RELIANT

Picture clue: Ready to plant

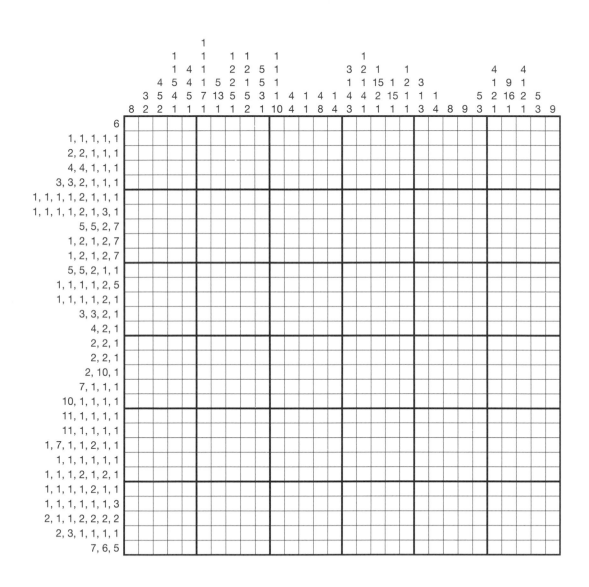

63: Spot the Difference

Solution on page 120

There are 10 differences to find.

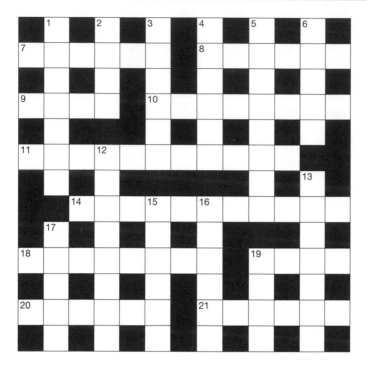

Across
7 Chinese martial art (4,2)
8 Voids (6)
9 Give up, as in power (4)
10 Military members (8)
11 Makes more difficult (11)
14 Acclaim for an achievement (11)
18 Written pieces (8)
19 Cans (4)
20 Rule (6)
21 Glowing ashes (6)

Down
1 Large piece of wood burned at
   Christmas (4,3)
2 Gawk at (4)
3 Oat-based breakfast food (6)
4 Spanish dish cooked in a shallow
   pan (6)
5 Occurrence (8)
6 Warning sound (5)
12 Placed in front, as in words (8)
13 Nation (7)
15 Hooked up to the Internet (6)
16 Chows down (6)
17 Criminal fire-starting (5)
19 Pipe (4)

I	Y	L	Y	R	T	E	O	P	E	I	L	A	D	N
W	K	L	R	O	E	P	A	I	N	T	I	N	G	S
Y	A	M	I	C	O	S	I	T	F	Y	U	O	S	L
O	A	L	A	M	Q	T	I	U	R	A	R	P	N	A
S	A	A	K	N	A	U	N	C	S	E	S	L	O	M
T	T	F	E	S	O	F	O	D	R	T	E	O	I	I
E	L	S	K	O	O	B	N	T	A	E	O	S	T	N
P	N	O	I	G	I	L	E	R	E	N	X	U	A	A
G	L	P	R	F	Y	D	S	T	C	S	C	E	S	E
E	E	I	L	C	R	C	L	O	U	D	S	E	R	X
R	V	C	S	A	I	I	E	P	S	P	N	O	E	E
C	A	E	S	W	N	S	E	S	D	P	A	F	V	T
A	R	L	N	V	R	T	U	N	U	O	D	E	N	N
O	T	I	S	T	R	S	S	M	D	I	A	N	O	R
F	A	S	S	P	S	N	I	F	S	S	L	P	C	S

ANIMALS
BOOKS
CLOUDS
CONVERSATIONS
DANCE
EVENTS
EXERCISE
FAMILY
FRIENDS
MUSIC
PAINTINGS
PETS
PLANTS
POETRY
QUOTES
RELIGION
STARS
TRAVEL
TREES
WALKS

66: Colouring

Solution on
page 120

Join dots in increasing numerical order, starting each path at a star. Lift your pen each time you reach a hollow circle.

68: Spot the Difference

There are 10 differences to find.

69: Square Maze

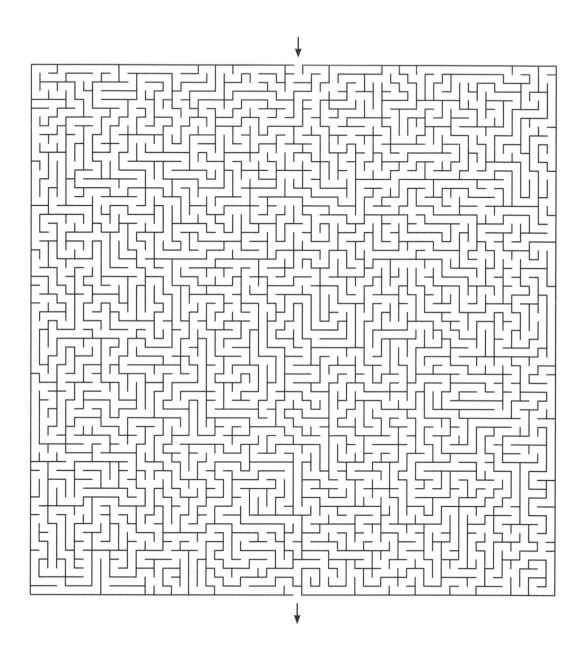

71: Crossword

Solution on page 121

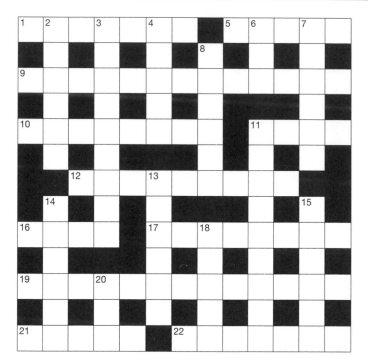

Across
1 Hostile (7)
5 Historical period (5)
9 Relating to matters of the mind (13)
10 Suggests (8)
11 Comply with (4)
12 Onlookers (9)
16 Hood (4)
17 Living-room display (2,6)
19 A kid's kids (13)
21 Even (5)
22 Mass per unit volume (7)

Down
2 Take a weapon away from (6)
3 Barring (9)
4 Type of footwear (5)
6 Letter following chi (3)
7 Volcano mouth (6)
8 Dwellings (6)
11 Changes a decision (9)
13 See (6)
14 Accusation (6)
15 Dislike (6)
18 'Look happy!' (5)
20 Born (3)

72: Peaceful Instruments

Solution on page 121

```
L D U L C I M E R E C I X R G
A T A N K D R U M H U A R E K
B R O L G O N G N U E I E K C
X J H K A L I M B A T H M A I
E O E D P A T I S R U A I H T
G K B D R E R N A B L N H S S
I H M I B O A O I E F G C R N
G V A M T P H A A L N U D V I
G C E N D U V C H L A H N P A
P J N N T H R O O S P H I R R
D C A A P A U H I N G G W A T
N H H K R I B A S C O N O H B
A N D I Z I T H E R E M I H E
A R U P N A T H S T M I H T C
C V N I A E E F R N K H O L N
```

BELL
DJEMBE
DULCIMER
GHANTA
GONG
HANDPANS
HANG
HARP
KALIMBA
MONOCHORD
PAN FLUTE
RAINSTICK
SHAKER
SHRUTI BOX
TANK DRUM
TANPURA
TINGSHA
VOICE
WIND CHIME
ZITHER

Join dots in increasing numerical order, starting each path at a star. Lift your pen each time you reach a hollow circle.

75: Dot to Dot

Join dots in increasing numerical order, starting each path at a star. Lift your pen each time you reach a hollow circle.

Join dots in increasing numerical order, starting each path at a star. Lift your pen each time you reach a hollow circle.

Solution on page 122

			3	9	7			
	1		4		6		2	
		6		2		7		
9	7						6	1
4		8				3		5
2	5						4	9
		2		3		4		
	8		2		9		3	
			8	6	4			

Solution on page 122

3				8				5
	6		5		3		9	
		5				8		
	5		7		9		4	
2				4				3
	7		8		2		1	
		2				1		
	9		4		6		5	
6				7				9

Join dots in increasing numerical order, starting each path at a star. Lift your pen each time you reach a hollow circle.

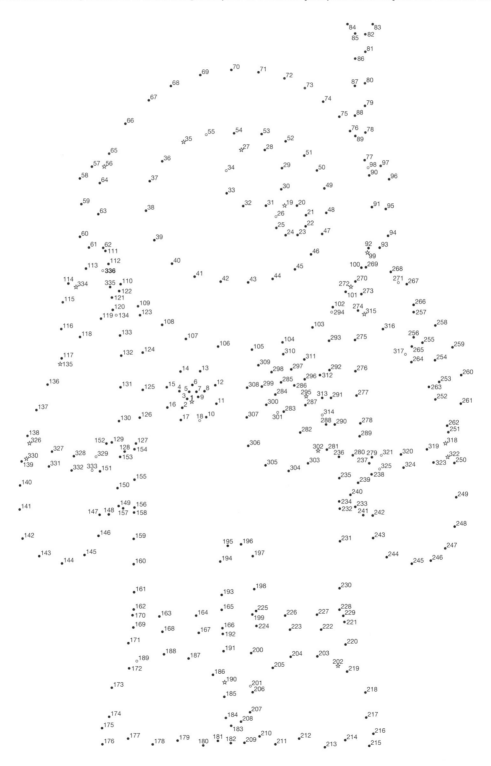

Solution on page 122

Picture clue: Feeling artistic

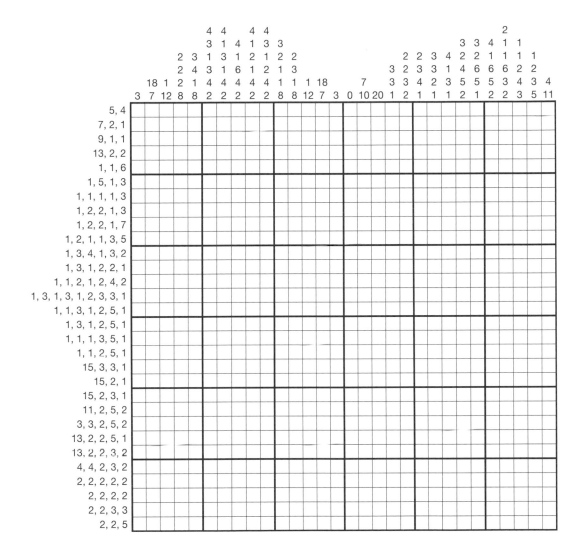

Join dots in increasing numerical order, starting each path at a star. Lift your pen each time you reach a hollow circle.

2			4		7			6
		8		5		2		
	3		9		2		7	
3		9				7		1
	5						9	
7		2				3		4
	2		8		6		4	
		6		7		8		
8			5		4			3

2			5	3	9			4
	9						3	
				4				
1				7				2
4		3	1		2	9		7
9				8				5
				2				
	1						7	
6			3	9	4			8

88: Dot to Dot

Solution on page 123

Join dots in increasing numerical order, starting each path at a star. Lift your pen each time you reach a hollow circle.

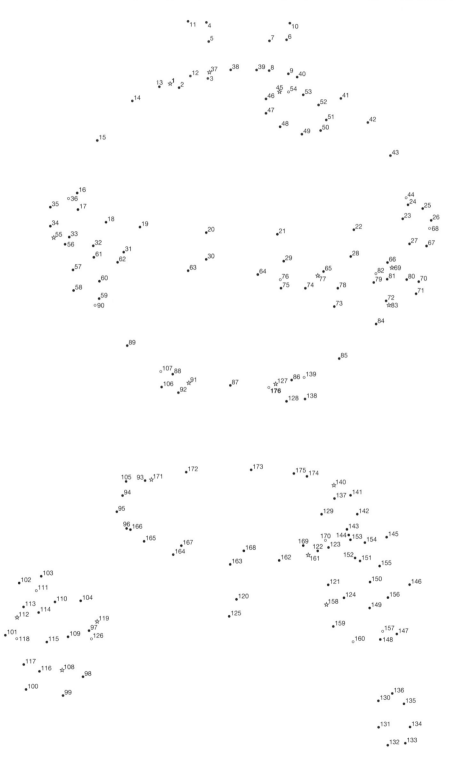

89: Take Your Time

Solution on page 123

```
C E C A P S G N I H T A E R B
N A E I T S T R E S P I T E D
O T T N T S T A N D S T I L L
I N A C O L T L I A T R I A P
S E E N H I U N U N C S D A U
N M T O O Y S L E T H J T E W
E E S E S I O S L M O A T H O
P N S I K R S U I U R C L T F
S O E K F I I S R M E E I T R
U P C A L L R N I B R O F L I
S T E E L L M T S M R E E E R
T S R R U E I G S E E E T T D
S O T B N H A D E T H R A N E
E P M T E D U L R E T N I T I
R S T O P P A G E E S U A P H
```

ADJOURNMENT
BREAK
BREATHING SPACE
CATCH YOUR BREATH
DEFERMENT
HALT
INTERLUDE
INTERMISSION
LULL
PAUSE
POSTPONEMENT
RECESS
REMISSION
RESPITE
REST
STANDSTILL
STOPPAGE
STRIKE
SUSPENSION
WAIT

90: Works of Art

Solution on page 123

```
N S G S K W A H T H G I N E T
T U A T D A V I D T S S I H A
H N C U E E D E H R T D E R M
E F I P H I B E E A N B E O E
U L N E L Y K H R U I K M P R
M O R F M I T R M R N R A H I
B W E H S A Y R T I B S E E C
R E U S B N O H H S E S R L A
E R G E I T O T E V E V C I N
L S H G A F E I N T T A S A G
L T H V V H Y T I R E V E G O
A T L E T S R E V O L E H T T
S A N M O N A L I S A T T E H
S U O O L I M E D S U N E V I
S R E P P U S T S A L E H T C
```

AMERICAN GOTHIC
DAVID
GUERNICA
MONA LISA
MY BED
NIGHTHAWKS
OPHELIA
SALVATOR MUNDI
STARRY NIGHT
SUNFLOWERS
THE BATHERS
THE BIRTH OF VENUS
THE KISS
THE LAST SUPPER
THE LOVERS
THE SCREAM
THE THINKER
THE UMBRELLAS
VENUS DE MILO
VERITY

Solution on
page 123

Join dots in increasing numerical order, starting each path at a star. Lift your pen each time you reach a hollow circle.

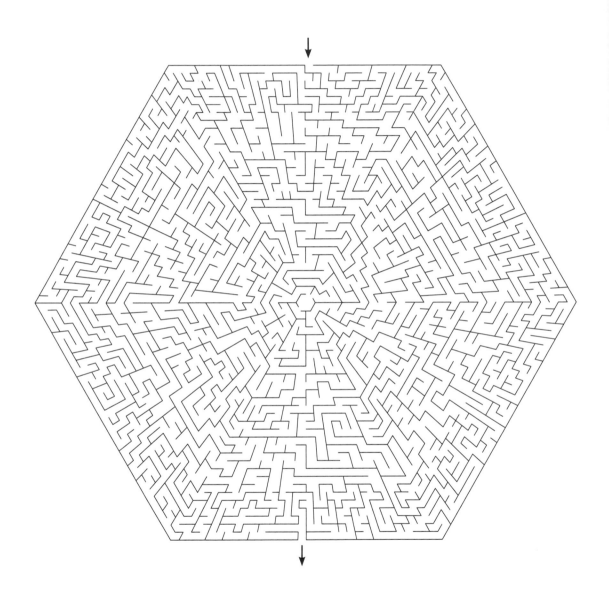

94: Dot to Dot

Join dots in increasing numerical order, starting each path at a star. Lift your pen each time you reach a hollow circle.

There are 15 differences to find.

Join dots in increasing numerical order, starting each path at a star. Lift your pen each time you reach a hollow circle.

85

Solution on
page 124

Picture clue: Staying out

Column clues (top):

```
                1   2   2               2   2
            11  1   1   1   13          1   1   1
    1  11  11   3   5   3   2   4  15  16   2   4   1   2           1   2       3   4   8   7   6   2   1   2   1   4   4   1   2   1   2
    1   3   4   2   2   4   3   2   6   1   1   2   5   3   8   6   2   8   1   2   1   1   1   1   1   1   1   1   1   1   1   1   1   1
    3   2   1   1   1   1   1   1   1   1   1   2   3   7   9  12  15   2  10  19  17  14  12   9   7   6   5   3   3   3   3   3   3   3
```

Row clues (left):

```
1, 2
2, 3
2, 6, 1
3, 8, 3
7, 2, 3, 6
14, 2, 3, 2
3, 3, 6, 3, 2
3, 3, 3, 3, 2
3, 3, 2
3, 3, 2, 18
3, 3, 2, 1, 1
3, 3, 2, 1, 1
3, 3, 1, 1, 2
3, 3, 2, 2, 2
3, 3, 1, 2, 2
14, 3, 3
3, 3
2, 4
3, 5
3, 5
4, 6
4, 6
5, 7
1, 6, 7
2, 6, 7
2, 1, 7, 8
6, 25
3, 3, 19
2, 2, 15
2, 1, 1, 2
3, 2, 4, 2
2, 6, 2
1, 4, 1
2, 2
11
```

99: Crossword

Solution on page 124

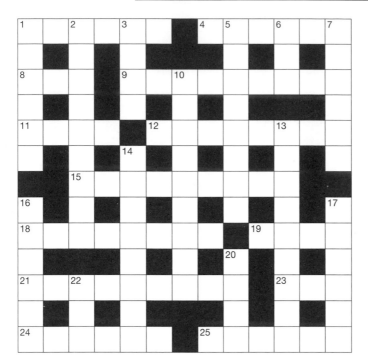

Across
1 For all of a given time interval (6)
4 Hurt (6)
8 Gratuity (3)
9 Vendors (9)
11 At any time (4)
12 Nastily (8)
15 Opinion piece (9)
18 Form the foundation of (8)
19 Party to (2,2)
21 Drowsy (9)
23 Anger (3)
24 Pick (6)
25 Joined (6)

Down
1 Obligations (6)
2 Criticize (9)
3 It's used for smelling (4)
5 Excessively sensitive (8)
6 Grow old (3)
7 Writings (6)
10 Advancing (9)
13 Equalizing (9)
14 Scans some text incorrectly (8)
16 In open view (6)
17 Text that has not been looked at (6)
20 Summit (4)
22 Noah's per-species limit (3)

100: A Walk in the Park

Solution on page 125

```
P S T N A L P R G T C S S G S
B D P A T H S C S P Y R N O E
S I N C O S R F L O W E R S P
S R R U W U P R T M Y G P F O
T S Y D O U T F A M S G L E L
R R D S S R E D E I E O S E S
E F O D S N G R O N L J I F R
E N B P P C R Y U O C I C R D
S T S I L C Y C A T R E N T A
I U M G R A S S I L P G S G L
Y E U T A T S P D N P L Y E S
U B U S H E S Y B S C G U M R
O I U T M A E R T S Y I S C F
E P O N D R U L S D S R P O S
C P R L G A R D E N E R C S E
```

BIRDS
BUSHES
CYCLISTS
FENCES
FLOWERS
GARDENER
GRASS
JOGGERS
OUTDOOR GYM
PATHS
PICNIC
PLANTS
PLAYGROUND
POND
RAILINGS
SCULPTURE
SLOPES
STATUE
STREAM
TREES

102: Spot the Difference

Solution on
page 125

There are 15 differences to find.

Across
1 Muscular tissue (5)
4 Principles (6)
10 Proscribed (9)
11 Something for a child to play with (3)
12 By surprise, as in 'taken ___' (5)
13 Thick-tipped pen (6)
14 Not available for use (3,2,6)
18 Complete disaster (6)
20 Madcap act (5)
23 Hawaiian floral garland (3)
24 Divide into parts (5,4)
25 Long-haired goat wool (6)
26 Adjust (5)

Down
2 Immature insect stage (5)
3 Continue doing (5,2)
5 Buffet car (5)
6 1920s decorative style (3,4)
7 States (4)
8 Butcher's leftovers (5)
9 Extremely common (1,4,1,5)
15 Joining (7)
16 Expressed gratitude (7)
17 Examines closely (5)
19 Not drunk (5)
21 Group of soldiers (5)
22 Supplication (4)

```
C E O E L A V E N D E R V E E
R M S E N T H Y M E U R A N I
N O N B N T G N O M A N N I C
R L W L E I S N L E U D I P N
O O N R G E M C B A S I L R R
T G R L E S L S C C B G L G E
S L E A G W E M A L S V A V N
C E N M N B O P Y J G E O V S
I N I I T G A L I N T L I M L
N G V M A U E Y F A C O L V G
A I L O R E N N E R L E G A S
L N E E F S I E U E E R A V L
V G M B E I S O T R H D O R D
N E O E T O M A G R E B L H R
S R N N C E D A R L N N E E M
```

BASIL
BAY
BERGAMOT
CEDAR
CINNAMON
CLOVE
ELDERFLOWER
GINGER
JASMINE
LAVENDER
LEMON
NEROLI
NUTMEG
ORANGE
PINE
ROSE
SAGE
THYME
VANILLA
VIOLET

Picture clue: Friendly hug

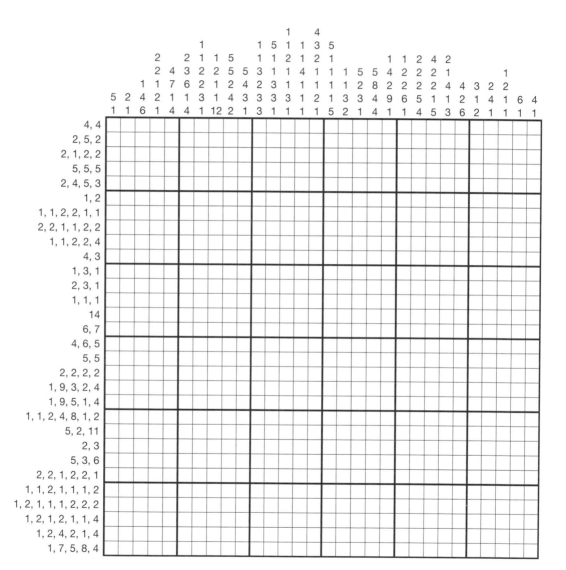

There are 15 differences to find.

Solution on
page 126

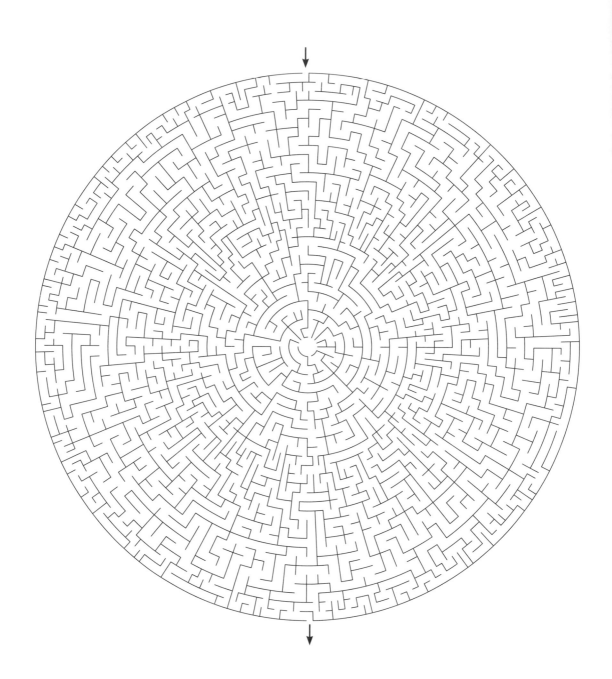

111: Dot to Dot

Join dots in increasing numerical order, starting each path at a star. Lift your pen each time you reach a hollow circle.

Picture clue: Sign of Love

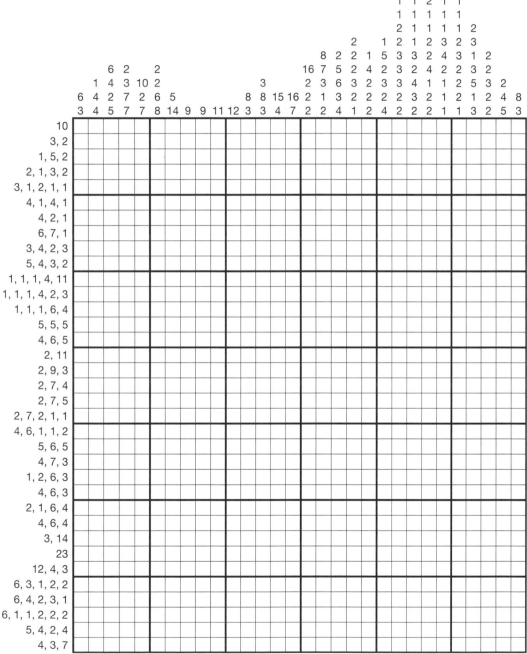

114: Spot the Difference

There are 15 differences to find.

Solution on
page 126

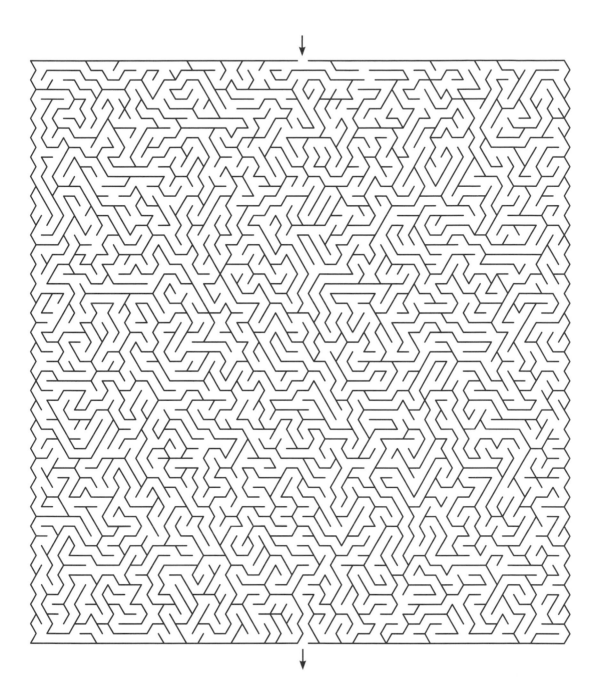

There are 15 differences to find.

Solution on
page 127

Join dots in increasing numerical order, starting each path at a star. Lift your pen each time you reach a hollow circle.

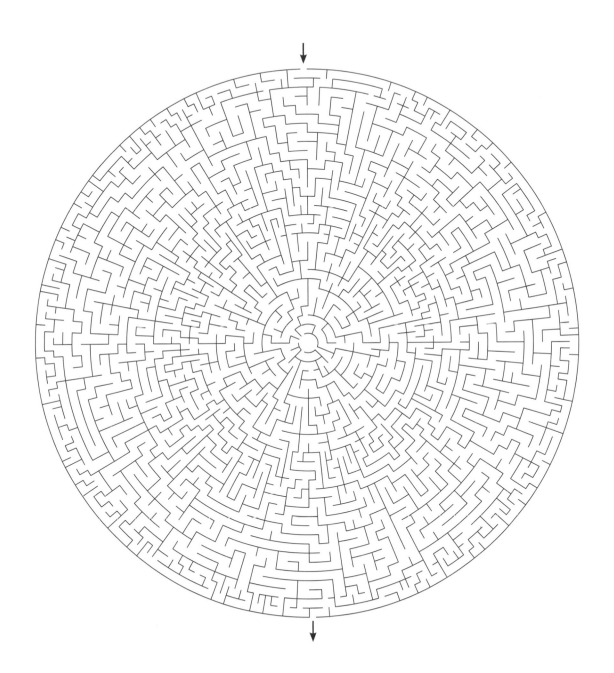

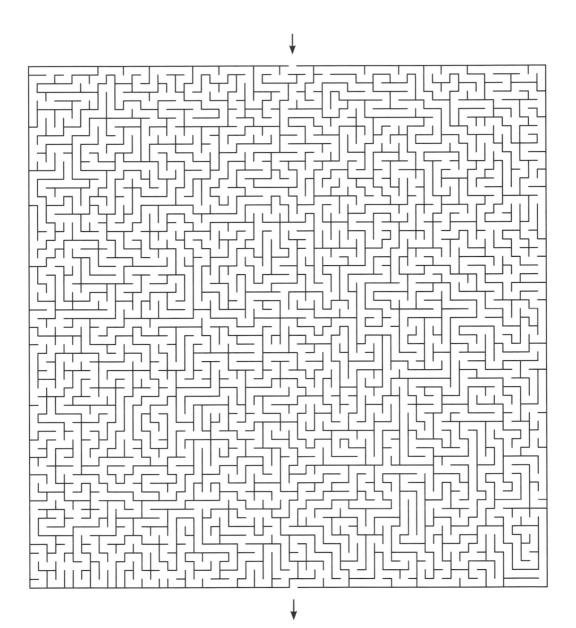

123: Spot the Difference

Solution on page 127

There are 20 differences to find.

Solution on
page 127

125: Sudoku

1			6		9			7
				1				
		9	7		2	4		
5		8		7		6		4
	1		8		3		9	
2		7		5		8		1
		5	1		4	3		
				6				
9			2		7			6

126: Sudoku

				7				
	5	3				2	8	
	6	9				3	4	
			1	8	6			
8			7		3			2
			2	9	5			
	3	1				7	9	
	7	4				8	6	
				5				

Solutions

Watering can

2

3

4

5

2	6	4	8	5	7	9	3	1
5	1	7	9	3	2	6	8	4
8	9	3	1	4	6	7	2	5
9	7	2	4	1	3	5	6	8
1	3	8	7	6	5	4	9	2
4	5	6	2	8	9	1	7	3
7	4	1	6	2	8	3	5	9
3	2	9	5	7	1	8	4	6
6	8	5	3	9	4	2	1	7

6

1	7	9	4	8	6	3	2	5
6	4	5	3	2	7	9	8	1
2	3	8	1	5	9	6	4	7
4	8	1	6	3	2	7	5	9
9	5	6	7	1	8	4	3	2
7	2	3	9	4	5	1	6	8
3	1	2	8	7	4	5	9	6
5	9	4	2	6	1	8	7	3
8	6	7	5	9	3	2	1	4

8

Barbecuing

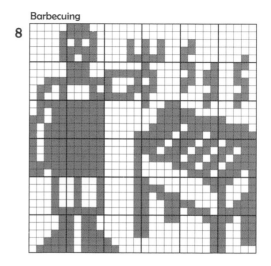

Solutions

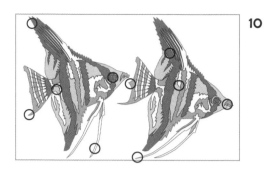

10

11

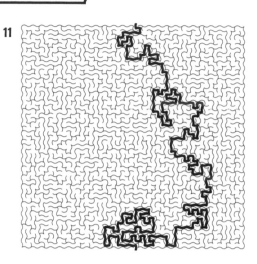

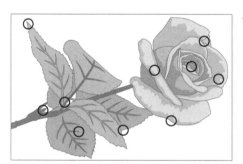

13

14

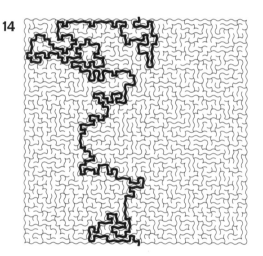

15

17

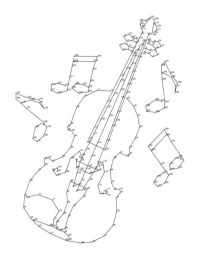

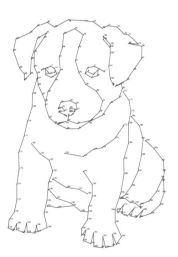

Solutions

19

21

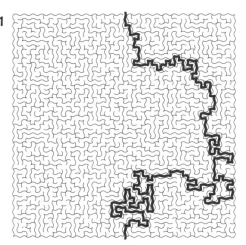

23

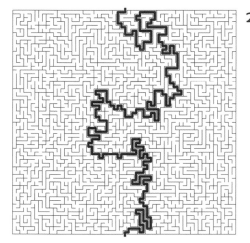

25

26

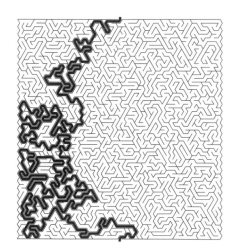

27

O		I		M		A		T		A		U
R	A	N	G	I	N	G		A	N	G	S	T
A		S		L		A	B		U			T
T	U	T	T	I		R	E	L	I	E	V	E
E		I		E			E					R
	U	N	S	U	C	C	E	S	S	F	U	L
R		C		U			U		O			Y
E	N	T	R	E	P	R	E	N	E	U	R	
P			M			E		L			B
O	B	E	Y	I	N	G		W	I	P	E	R
R		D		G		U		E		L		U
T	I	G	E	R		M	I	S	S	A	L	S
S		E		E		S		T		Y		H

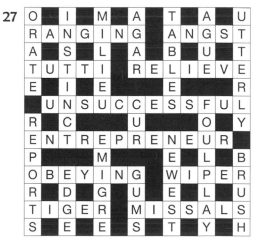

Solutions

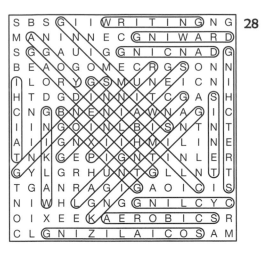

28

30 Jigsaw puzzle

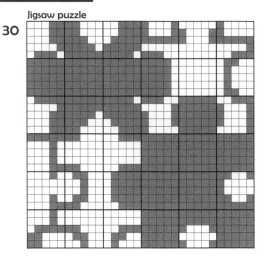

32 Seashell

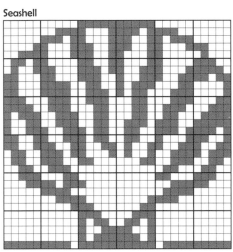

33

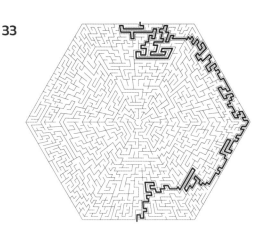

34

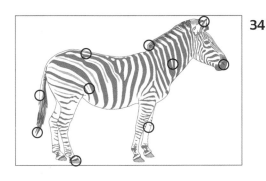

36

4	9	5	8	7	1	6	2	3
6	8	7	9	2	3	5	4	1
2	1	3	6	5	4	8	9	7
7	6	4	3	9	2	1	8	5
1	3	8	5	4	7	9	6	2
9	5	2	1	8	6	3	7	4
3	4	6	7	1	9	2	5	8
8	7	9	2	3	5	4	1	6
5	2	1	4	6	8	7	3	9

Solutions

37

8	4	7	9	6	3	5	2	1
3	5	9	2	1	4	7	8	6
1	2	6	7	8	5	4	3	9
6	8	2	4	3	9	1	7	5
4	1	3	5	7	6	8	9	2
9	7	5	8	2	1	3	6	4
5	3	4	6	9	8	2	1	7
7	6	1	3	5	2	9	4	8
2	9	8	1	4	7	6	5	3

38

Hot-air balloon

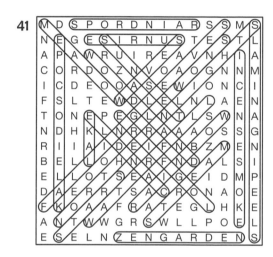

40

EVES SCENARIO
PRETTY CODING
PURR INTERNAL
BLACKANDWHITE
SYMPATHY PATS
NIPPLE HAIRDO
ESPRESSO RUST

41

43

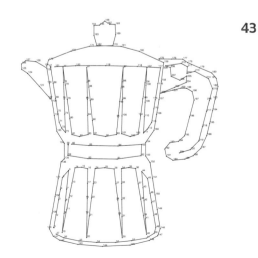

44

KNUCKLEDOWN
SELFMOTIVATED
LEISURED IDLE
AVIAN NAVAL
EAST PROLONGS
BUBONICPLAGUE
RECONDITION

Solutions

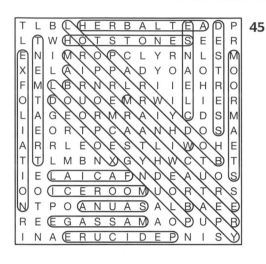

45

47

9	4	6	5	8	1	7	3	2
1	7	3	9	4	2	6	5	8
5	2	8	6	3	7	1	9	4
7	9	1	3	6	4	2	8	5
6	8	5	1	2	9	4	7	3
4	3	2	7	5	8	9	6	1
8	1	7	2	9	3	5	4	6
3	5	9	4	1	6	8	2	7
2	6	4	8	7	5	3	1	9

48

4	1	2	9	8	5	3	6	7
5	8	6	3	1	7	2	9	4
3	7	9	6	4	2	8	1	5
8	2	4	5	9	1	6	7	3
9	5	7	8	6	3	1	4	2
1	6	3	2	7	4	5	8	9
6	3	1	7	2	9	4	5	8
2	9	8	4	5	6	7	3	1
7	4	5	1	3	8	9	2	6

49

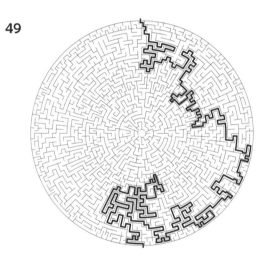

51

B	E	E	F	Y	█	T	E	R	R	I	F	Y
█	Q	█	L	█	P	█	A	█	I	█	R	█
A	U	T	O	C	R	A	T	█	F	E	E	S
█	I	█	W	█	E	█	H	█	L	█	E	█
U	P	K	E	E	P	█	U	P	E	N	D	█
█	█	█	R	█	A	█	M	█	O	█	█	█
T	H	I	S	█	R	I	B	█	H	Y	M	N
█	A	█	█	█	A	█	L	█	O	█	█	█
█	S	M	A	R	T	█	E	N	L	A	C	E
█	B	█	N	█	I	█	P	█	D	█	O	█
S	E	M	I	█	O	R	I	G	I	N	A	L
█	E	█	M	█	N	█	E	█	N	█	S	█
E	N	M	A	S	S	E	█	█	A	G	A	T	E

52

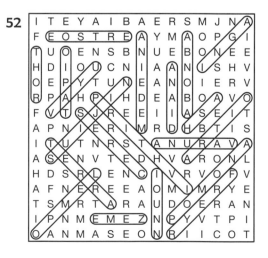

118

54

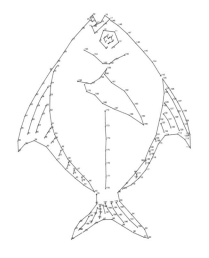

55

	A	C	R	I	D		S	P	E	E	C	H
A		O		N		C		U		R		E
B	O	D	Y	C	L	O	C	K		O	A	F
U		E		L		N		K		S		T
S	U	S	H	I		S	T	A	S	I	S	
E				N		U				O		
		I	M	P	E	R	M	A	N	E	N	T
		O			P		O					C
		I	N	F	E	C	T		M	E	A	L	Y
S		I		B		I		A		W		S
H	O	T		B	R	O	A	D	C	A	S	T
I		O		E		N		I		R		S
P	A	R	A	D	E		S	C	U	D	S	

56

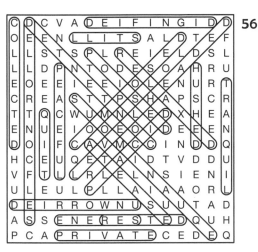

57

59

60

	O	P	T	I	C	A	L		L	O	I	N
A		O		M		N		M		P		E
C	H	E	A	P	L	Y		A	V	E	R	S
A		M		R		W		T		N		T
D	I	S	C	O		A	S	H	R	A	M	
E				V		Y		E		I		C
M	E	M	B	E	R		E	M	B	R	Y	O
Y		A		M		A		A				C
		I	N	V	E	N	T		T	O	R	C	H
A		K		N		E		I		E		L
J	O	I	N	T		M	A	C	H	I	N	E
A		N		S		P		A		G		A
R	I	D	E		F	O	O	L	I	N	G	

Solutions

61

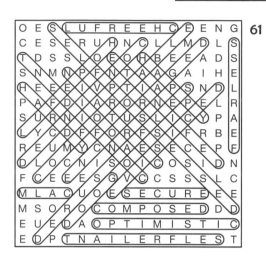

62

Pot and gardening tools

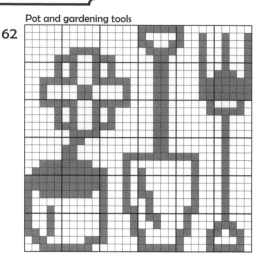

63

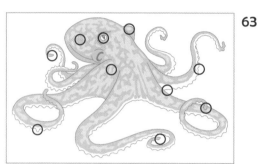

64

	Y		O		M		P	I		A	
K	U	N	G	F	U		A	N	N	U	L	S
	L		L		E		E		C		A	
C	E	D	E		S	O	L	D	I	E	R	S
	L		L		L		L	D			M	
C	O	M	P	L	I	C	A	T	E	S		
	G		R				N			C	
			R	E	C	O	G	N	I	T	I	O	N
	A		F		N	O				U	
A	R	T	I	C	L	E	S		T	I	N	S
	S		X		I		H		U		T	
G	O	V	E	R	N		E	M	B	E	R	S
	N		D		E		S		E		Y	

65

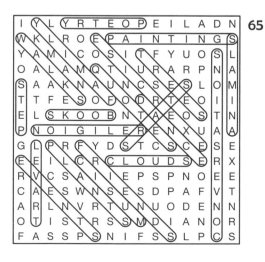

67

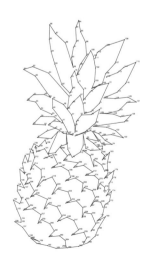

120

Solutions

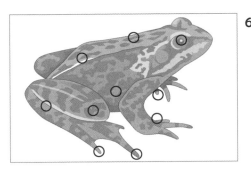 68

69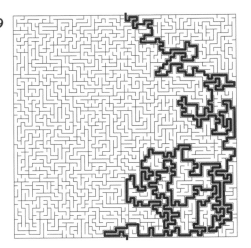

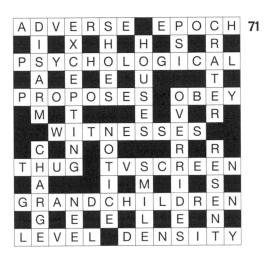 71

72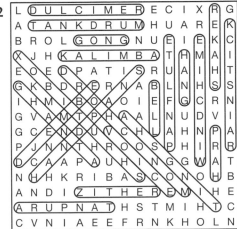

73 75

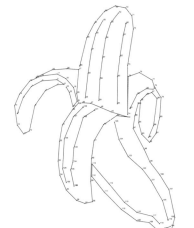 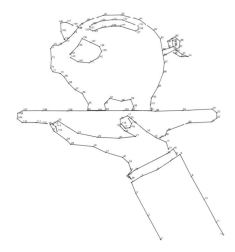

121

Solutions

77

78

8	2	5	3	9	7	6	1	4
7	1	9	4	8	6	5	2	3
3	4	6	1	2	5	7	9	8
9	7	3	5	4	8	2	6	1
4	6	8	9	1	2	3	7	5
2	5	1	6	7	3	8	4	9
5	9	2	7	3	1	4	8	6
6	8	4	2	5	9	1	3	7
1	3	7	8	6	4	9	5	2

79

3	1	7	9	8	4	6	2	5
8	6	4	5	2	3	7	9	1
9	2	5	1	6	7	8	3	4
1	5	6	7	3	9	2	4	8
2	8	9	6	4	1	5	7	3
4	7	3	8	5	2	9	1	6
5	4	2	3	9	8	1	6	7
7	9	8	4	1	6	3	5	2
6	3	1	2	7	5	4	8	9

81

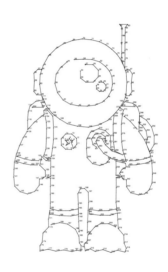

Easel and palette

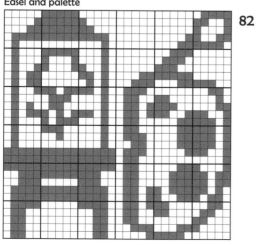

82

84

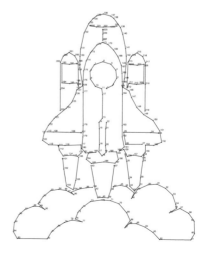

Solutions

2	9	1	4	8	7	5	3	6
4	7	8	6	5	3	2	1	9
6	3	5	9	1	2	4	7	8
3	6	9	2	4	5	7	8	1
1	5	4	7	3	8	6	9	2
7	8	2	1	6	9	3	5	4
5	2	3	8	9	6	1	4	7
9	4	6	3	7	1	8	2	5
8	1	7	5	2	4	9	6	3

85

86

2	6	1	5	3	9	7	8	4
7	9	4	2	1	8	5	3	6
5	3	8	6	4	7	2	9	1
1	5	6	9	7	3	8	4	2
4	8	3	1	5	2	9	6	7
9	2	7	4	8	6	3	1	5
8	4	9	7	2	1	6	5	3
3	1	2	8	6	5	4	7	9
6	7	5	3	9	4	1	2	8

88

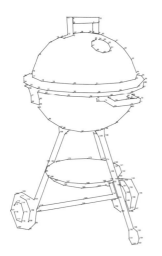

89

90

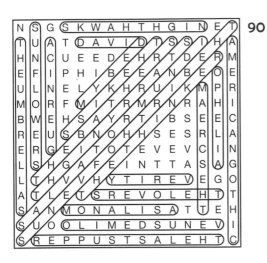

91

Solutions

93 **94**

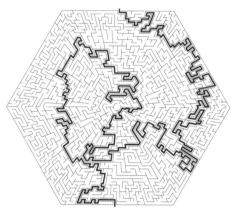

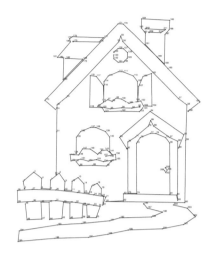

95 **96**

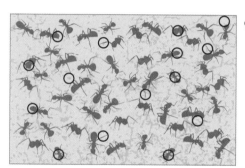

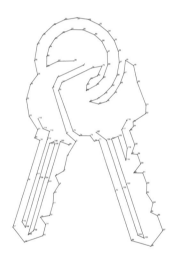

Campsite with tent

98 **99**

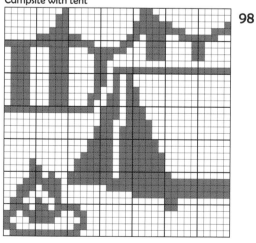

D	U	R	I	N	G			D	A	M	A	G	E
U		E		O				L		G			S
T	I	P		S	U	P	P	L	I	E	R	S	
I		R		E		R		E				A	
E	V	E	R		H	O	R	R	I	B	L	Y	
S		H		M		M		G		A			S
		E	D	I	T	O	R	I	A	L			
P		N		S		T		C		A			U
U	N	D	E	R	L	I	E			I	N	O	N
B			E		N		A			C			R
L	E	T	H	A	R	G	I	C			I	R	E
I		W		D			M			N			A
C	H	O	O	S	E		M	E	R	G	E	D	

Solutions

100

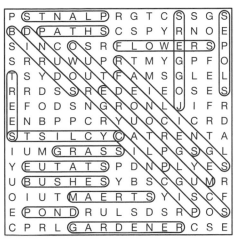

102

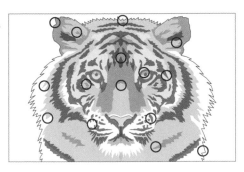

103

104

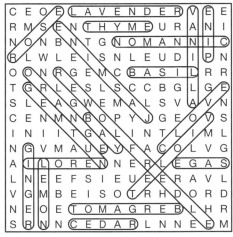

Cuddly toy

105

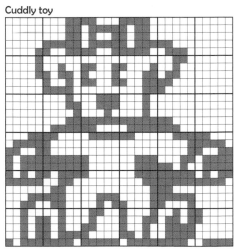

107

Solutions

109 **111**

Rose

113 **114**

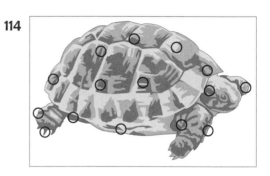

116 **117**

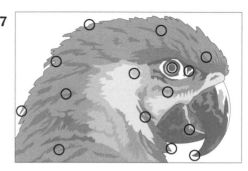